HIKING

FOR BEGINNERS

7 Steps to Becoming a Capable Hiker

ALAN GREENFIELD

Table of Contents

Introduction 6
Getting in Shape for Hiking 7
Develop a Training Schedule 8
The Three Basics 9
Types of Hiking Training.................................. 10
Step 1 13
   Choosing to Hike Alone or with a Group 14
   Choosing a Type of Hike 15
Step 2 19
   Choosing a Hiking Route and Trail 20
Step 3 29
   Choosing Appropriate Clothing 30
   What to Wear While Hiking............................ 30
   Choosing the Best Socks for Hiking 34
   Height 35
   Cushioning.. 36
   Fabric 38
   Fit 39
   Choosing Hiking Shoes or boots 40

Types 41
Components 42
Fit 46
Step 4 49
Choosing the Right Hiking Gear 50
The Eleven Essentials 50
Navigation 52
Sun Protection 53
Insulation 54
Illumination 54
First-Aid Supplies 55
Fire 56
Tools and Repair Kit 56
Nutrition 56
Bug Protection 57
Hydration 57
Emergency Shelter 58
Step 5 61
Choosing and Preparing Food and Water 62
Nutritional Information 63
When to Eat 65
Types 67
Water 69

Step 6 77
- Preparing for Hiking Safety and Emergencies .. 78
- Hiking in the Winter 78
- Hiking in the Summer 80
- Read a Map and Use a Compass 80
- Water Purification 81
- What to Do If You Get Lost 82
- First Aid while Hiking 86
- Blisters 87

Step 7 93
- The Hike - Proper Etiquette 94
- Right of Way 94
- Leave No Trace 95
- Give Back 96

A Note From the Author 98

Resources 99

INTRODUCTION

Great views, fresh air, wildlife, and the scent of pine trees and green grass. Getting outside is rejuvenating, inspiring, and good for your fitness.

Hiking is one of the most widely-available outdoors pursuits for people across the world. According to the Physical Activity Council, hiking is a Top 10 sports and fitness activity across all segments of the popultion.

When you need a true break – a mental disconnect -- it is time to head outdoors and get back to nature. Hiking is great for your body and your mind. With a little planning and activity, hiking is something anyone can do; even beginners who have never stepped foot on a trail before. Getting started as a beginner hiker isn't hard, you just need a little knowledge and preparation.This book is a beginner's guide that will help you get ready, plan your first hike and know what to expect when you get out there. So if you want to get started with hiking, keep reading and I'll show you how you can do it in 7 days. By next weekend, you will be hiking like an old pro!

Getting in Shape for Hiking

Before we get you into the 7 steps of hiking preparation, there is one thing you need to do that might require some prep time. Hiking requires some baseline level of fitness. While you don't have to be in perfect shape to go for a hike, you do need to be able to safely and competently complete the hikes that you select.

If you are not at a base level of fitness, spend a little time training for hiking and getting yourself in proper physical and mental shape before you head out on the trail. Preparation is key to increasing your chance for success and enjoyment while on the trail.

Keep in mind that different trails call for different levels of conditioning. Many flatter and short trails, with good footing, are great places for the novice and the person who is not in great shape to get exercise. But some trails are more difficult, requiring better stamina, strength, and agility. For those trails, be sure that you are in proper shape before heading out. Many state and local websites actually profile each trail to help tell you which type of fitness and skill level it is suitable for.

Let's look at how you can get in shape for hiking.

Develop a Training Schedule

The first thing you need to do when preparing is determine what type of hiking you plan to do. Are you going to be doing strenuous hiking on mountains that involves unsure footing and "scrambling" (climbing on all fours at times)? Or maybe you are going on an overnight hike in the wilderness that will require some additional stamina? Or perhaps you are simply going on a day hike in your local park, in a relatively flat trail. For any type of hike, you want to be in decent physical shape. However, there is a difference between the physical needs for a short day hike and an overnight wilderness trip.

One great benefit of hiking is that it will, by itself, get you into better shape than when you started. Don't worry too much about being in tip-top condition, just be sure you can handle the trails that you intend to tackle.

If you aren't a frequent hiker or walker you should start by making a habit of doing some activity, anything, several times a week. For a few weeks, give your legs daily exercise so you can set yourself up for a successful trip outside. Longer hikes and overnight trips are going to need additional training beyond basic exercise. Training for these hikes requires an exercise routine. For the purpose of this book we are only going to focus on the basics of a simple day hike and how to get in shape for it.

THE THREE BASICS

Hiking is a natural form of exercise for most people. Walking is a natural transportation method and it is an easy activity. However, this doesn't mean that everyone is prepared to hike long distances over a prolonged period of time. Most people need to do some form of training before heading out on a hike. There are three basics you need to do to get prepared.

First, you want to start doing some bodyweight exercises, or even gym exercises if you have access to one. The lunge is a great example, something that will help you build your leg strength. Bodyweight or gym exercises will help you to condition your body while helping to improve your stamina and strength. Start out by finding a routine you like, and doing it regularly. It doesn't have to be terribly complicated, you just need to stick to it.

Second, starting getting outdoors. The obvious thing is to start getting outdoors with small and easy walks. Consider starting with long walks at your local park or somewhere near your house. Gradually work to increase the length and elevation gain of your walks. This will help your body get accustomed to an actual hiking trip without jumping straight into one.

Third, improve your habits. This may be the hardest of all the preparation even though it seems the easiest. Basically you want to change your habits so you can get a little extra exercise in your daily routine. Other habits that are good for hiking but will also help your general help include things like drinking plenty of water, reducing the sugars and simple carbs from your diet, and eliminating cigarette use (if it applies) and reducing alcohol consumption. The first hike you do in a steep incline, or an exceptionally hot day, and your body will be thankful you are taking better care of yourself.

The great things about adopting these three preparation steps is that they will not only get you ready for hiking, but they should positively impact your health and fitness overall.

Types of Hiking Training

When you are learning to hike for the first time, or after a long period of not hiking, it is important to know the different types of training. There are three main areas you can focus on when training for hiking.

First, cardiovascular training. Cardio workouts are best for hiking training. The recommendation is to do two days of cardio workout for every single day of strength training. Three to four days a week is ideal. It is also best to have one day of rest per week to allow you to recover both mentally and physically. The goal of a cardio workout is to optimize your body's ability to recuperate. Cardio workouts also help to improve your endurance. Examples of cardio workouts including walking, jogging, swimming, cycling and fitness classes. The focus of cardio workouts is to push your body to the point of fatigue, yet never reach the point of exhaustion. You should start with light exercise to increase your heart rate and then gradually increase the duration and intensity.

Your cardio training does not have to be intense. In fact, just going for a brisk walk around your neighborhood can do. Studies have shown that doing some intervals of faster walking within a longer walk can accelerate your cardio benefits.

Second, resistance and strength training. The purpose of resistance training is to target specific muscle groups and parts of the body. This helps to teach your body how to manage prolonged physical stress. You should have at least two days of resistance training in your weekly schedule. Some good resistance exercises to try include squats, lunges, planks, step-ups, sit-ups and push-ups.

Third, mental training. Mentally preparing for a hike is just as important as the physical training. No matter what physical shape you are in, you can't be prepared for the adversity of hiking. As you increase the length of your hiking trips you can face problems such as cold weather, sudden downpours, gear issues and blisters among others. The only way to overcome these is through mental training. You are getting started with your mental training by reading this book so you will be adequately prepared and ready for your hike. So let's get started and look at how you can get ready for your first hike in a step by step guide that will take you through 7 steps of preparation.

STEP 1

Choosing to Hike Alone or with a Group

Experiencing the great outdoors on a hike by yourself provides the greatest feeling of freedom, because the great outdoors offers an adventure like no other. However, it can also be lonely and intimidating. For those new to hiking, it can often be a good idea to start out doing it with others. This way you have someone there to help if something goes wrong, not to mention having someone to help inspire you to keep going during the difficult stretches.

Where can you find a hiking partner? If you don't know of anyone who would like to hike with you then you can find hiking groups and communities online.. Many cities have hiking clubs that have regular outings you can join. You can also look for local hiking classes and events, at outfitters and outdoors shops.

Hiking in solitude can be great as well, just know you need to be self-sufficient on the trial. If you really want to go hiking on your own, remember to practice hiking safety. Always tell someone where you plan to hike and how long you plan to be gone. This way you have someone to look out for you if you don't return at the designated time and can contact help for you.

Once you know whether you are hiking alone or in a group, the next thing you need to do on your first day is to determine what type of hiking you are going to do and what you need to be prepared.

Do bring your cell phone as a backup plan, but don't overly rely on it. A cell phone does not always work well on trails in more rugged areas.

Choosing a Type of Hike

When I ask what type of hiking people want to do I often get a confused look. After all, isn't hiking a single activity? While the physical act of hiking isn't going to change, there are different reasons and types of hikes to consider. Let's look at the types of hikes available so you can see what I mean and get an idea of what you want to do.

Types of Hiking

Day Hikes

Day hikes are, far and away, the most popular type of hikes done by hikers all around the world.

For a beginning hiker, the day hike is the best way to start building your hiking skills. For a day hike you should choose a well marked and maintained trail that is near to your home. Be sure to research the trail before you go to see how much time and effort the trail will take. We'll discuss this in greater detail in the next chapter on choosing a hike and trail. Even though you are only taking a day hike, you want to make sure you pack the eleven essentials and we'll look at this later under choosing appropriate gear. Once you gain more experience you may want to consider some other types of hiking.

Note that some hikes are "out-and-back" hikes, meaning you will hike the same trail back as you did out to your destination. Others are "loop" hikes where you will do some type of route other than out-and-back. If you do a loop hike, just be sure you have the time and energy to do the whole thing. On an out-and-back hike, it is easier to simply turn around if you find yourself losing steam.

Overnight Hikes

Once you have more experience, you'll also have developed a favorite set of hiking spots. Why not consider spending more time in your favorite spot by going on an overnight hiking adventure, especially if it is one that is setup to accommodate camping hikers. This will require a little more time and planning as well as more focus on safety and comfort.

An overnight hike can be a great way to test the waters for a more extensive, backpacking type of hike. For an overnight, you will need to make sure you have sleeping and basic meals covered, but it is not as complex as a multi-day trip.

From here you can move up to another level of hiking.

Backpacking

An extended hiking trip is known as backpacking and often includes more than a few days outdoors. For these trips you need excellent hiking skills, strength and extensive planning. However, if you want to really explore the outdoors then you'll get the greatest benefits and experience from a multi-day backpacking experience.

Within these three types of hiking there are multiple different options you can do to make each hiking experience unique and enjoyable.

For the day hiker a fun alternative is to try geocaching. With this option you hike with the purpose of finding a secret, hidden cache that only those with a navigational unit like a GPS and coordinates can find.

With experience perhaps you could consider taking a hike at night. Night hiking isn't for everyone and will require some additional skill and planning.

If you have an interest in mind, consider making your day hike a pilgrimage. Visit a historic region or site. This way you can experience nature and history at the same time, and there will be a clear destination for you to measure your hike by.

STEP 2

Choosing a Hiking Route and Trail

Once you've decided the type of hiking you want to do and whether you are going to do it alone or as a group, the next set of decisions focus on where to hike. This is a critical decision, because choosing the right trail will have a huge impact on your overall experience Choose something too difficult, and you could get discouraged. Choose something too easy, and you might not get the thrill the comes with challenging yourself.

There are a few ways that you can find a hiking trail to meet your interests. Guidebooks and websites are your best option since they give you all the information you need including the following:

- Difficulty
- Distance
- Elevation Gain
- Directions
- Trail Features

Websites will also often give you the added benefit of getting current trail conditions. One of our favorite is AllTrails, a site that allows users to enter their impressions of each trail. We like looking up reviews from the same time of year as our intended hike, so that we get an idea of how the hike will be during that exact season.

Another option is to find out from others. If you know someone who likes to hike you can talk with them and get some tips on where to go for your first hiking adventure. If you don't know of anyone then you can consider talking to the locals. You can often find a local hiking organization or a ranger station in the area that can give you advice on the best hikes for beginners. Ranger stations can also be a good source of up to the minute trail conditions.

Once you have several suggestions for the best beginner hikes in the area then you need to consider trail types and difficulty. When you look at hikes you'll often see a "trail type" as a category in the information. The following are the most common trail types and what they mean:

- Loop Trail: These trails start and end at the same place without any part of the trail repeating itself. They are great and interesting, but don't get caught a the apex of a loop with no energy or water left.
- Out and Back Trail: These trails require you to hike to an end point and then return the same way you came. The walk back might be less interesting because you are backtracking, but an advantage is that you can make these hikes

as long as you want -- just turn around when you are ready.
- Point to Point Trail: These trails often have more than one trailhead and/or access point since they are often several miles long. For experienced hikers with the stamina, you can hike to the end and then back to where you started. You can also arrange for pickup at another point and get a ride back to your vehicle if you don't want to repeat any part of the trail.
- Semi Loop Trail: These trails have you hike out to a loop and then you repeat the first part of the trail back to the trailhead where you started after completing the loop.
- Interpretive Trail: These are often short and easy nature hikes with educational signs to stop and read along the way with information about local history, wildlife and flora.
- Spur Trail: These are short trails that often branch off from a main trail and typically take you to a special feature or scenic viewpoint.

There may be other types of trails out there, but these are the most common you'll run into as a beginning hiker. In addition to the type of trail, you'll also want to consider the trail difficulty.

A mile is a measurement, but it isn't the same distance when you consider walking versus hiking.

If you are hiking you need to consider additional factors such as the following:

- Elevation Gain
- Obstacles
- Length
- Seasonal Issues

Let's consider these in detail so you know what to consider when choosing a hiking trail.

Elevation gain is something important to research before hiking. Climbs or descents can be difficult for any injuries you have such as bad knees. You need to focus both on the elevation gain throughout the hike as well as how quickly the elevation gain happens. For example, an elevation gain over 5 miles of 1,000 feet isn't that difficult; but the same gain over a mile distance can be far more difficult and challenging. As a beginner, if you aren't in the best of shape then you should choose trails that have a minimum elevation gain or gentle switchbacks to make the hike more tolerable for you.

Trail length is another thing you want to consider, but first you need to determine what length of trail you are comfortable with. The length of trail you are comfortable with will depend on your fitness level and how long you have to be out hiking. A general rule of thumb to follow is that hiking takes 20 minutes per mile on a flat and easy trail. If you have difficult or steep terrain, weather conditions and/or plan to take a break for eating then you are going to need a longer baseline. As a beginner you should choose shorter hikes you know you can handle.

Next, you want to consider trail obstacles that you are likely to encounter along the way such as boulders, mud, downed trees, etc. You should especially look for any streams you have to cross if there are no bridges. Crossing water obstacles is dangerous and requires special effort. In general, know the footing that you will have, and be sure to dress appropriately. We have hiked on trails that are paved and nearly flat, and others that at times required us to be on all fours, "scrambling" up a large rock (but stopping short of rock-climbing).

Seasons can also affect your hiking. The season you are hiking in will drastically impact the landscape. The first thing you need to do is check to ensure the trail you choose is open year-round. Also keep in mind the fact that you have less daylight hours when hiking in fall and winter compared to the summer. Before you leave to go on your hike you should always check the weather forecast since large storms can make hiking dangerous and some trails may even become inaccessible.

Most of all you want to choose a trail to hike that inspires you and doesn't intimidate you.

There are plenty of beautiful trails to hike and a lot work for beginners. It is important that you start small and simple and work your way up to the longer and more challenging hikes as you gain experience, strength and stamina.

As you start looking for a hike using the above research there are also a few tips you want to use when choosing a hike. Keep the following in mind to help you choose the best hike as a beginner.

First, know how much time you have. Do you only have a few hours or do you have the entire day to spend outdoors hiking? The amount of time you can spend hiking outdoors will have a big impact on where you can go. You should also remember to factor in how long it will take you to get to and from the trailhead.

Also keep in mind your fitness level. Make an honest assessment of the shape you're in since you want to have an enjoyable time rather than suffering through a long and strenuous hike that you weren't prepared for. Don't be discouraged if you aren't in the best of shape, you'll work your way there. That's why you're hiking after all. The purpose is to keep it enjoyable so you'll want to keep hiking rather than give up because it is too difficult.

You also want to think about distance. While the time and fitness level is going to factor big into the distance you are going to be able to travel; you also want to consider how many miles you are comfortable hiking. The average walking pace is three miles per hour, but hiking can be much slower based on terrain, elevation gain and how much gear you are carrying.

As we discussed above, elevation gain is also important to consider. The elevation gain is the biggest determining factor in the difficulty of the trail. It is best to keep your beginning hikes to little or no elevation gain and then learn how much elevation gain you can comfortably handle as you gain experience. A general rule of thumb is that for every 1,000 feet of elevation gain you should add an extra hour on your hike.

Another thing to consider is the weather and time of year you are hiking. Some trails are only available in certain times of the year and closed in others. If you are hiking in the fall, plan accordingly so you don't get caught outside after dark. Checking the weather forecast means you can dress appropriately and pack the right gear. If you are hiking in an area known for thunderstorms or snow, be especially sure to know the weather before heading out. We can tell you from experience that getting caught on a trail during a thunderstorm is a very helpless feeling.

Lastly, you want to consider logistics. Some hikes require more planning than others. For example, if you plan on doing a hike that starts and finishes in different locations then you need to plan for shuttle cars at each point.

Once you've finished planning your hike you will know what you need to prepare for it. Let's move on to how you can prepare for your hike with the next four days of hiking for beginners. The third step is going to focus on choosing the appropriate clothing for your hike.

STEP 3

Choosing Appropriate Clothing

Fortunately, hiking tends to not be an expensive hobby, but one of the most important things you will invest in when hiking is clothing. While you may think you simply need to put on some comfortable clothing from your closet and head out on the trail, it isn't that simple. There is a lot of thought and planning that goes into choosing the appropriate clothing for hiking. Let's take a look at why this part of planning for hiking requires a full day.

What to Wear While Hiking

When hiking, we recommend choosing clothing that is made from quick-drying and moisture-wicking fabrics. The best options are wool or polyester. Contrary to popular belief, you should avoid clothing made from cotton since they take a long time to dry once they get wet. When choosing what to wear while hiking you want to think of your clothing as separate systems:

- Skin Base Layers: In cool to cold climates you want to wear clothing made of wool or polyester on clothing that is next to your skin.
- Hiking Layers: When hiking it is important that you dress in layers to adjust to a variety of conditions and climate changes. These layers

should include nylon and/or polyester pants, shirt, sun shirt and hat.
- Insulation Layers: Depending on how cold the climate you are hiking in, you should have an insulation layer such as a puffy vest or jacket, lightweight fleece pullover and/or warm hat and gloves.
- Rainwear Layers: Lastly, if you are going to be hiking in wet weather you want to have a waterproof jacket and/or rain pants.

Obviously, your normal hiking conditions will play a major factor in the clothing you should invest in. If you will be hiking in an area that is known for cool rain, you will want to invest more in rain gear than someone who might spend most of their time hiking in an area known for dry sunshine. If you are hiking in a climate that gets hot and humid, you need to focus more on breathable and moisture-wicking gear. If you might be hiking in a cold northern climate, you will need to invest more in your base layers and insulation.

Let's look at some of these clothing options in more detail so you can dress appropriately when hiking.

When it comes to choosing pants/shorts, the best deciding factor is your environment. If the weather forecast is too cold then shorts won't keep you warm enough, but if the forecast is hot then pants might keep you too warm. The most important thing to remember is to avoid wearing jeans. You should only wear jeans hiking if it is going to be a comfortable temperature and you have no other clothing options. It is best to choose pants made from lightweight materials that dry quickly.

Many hikers assume that if it is a comfortable, mild day, they should wear shorts. We advise against shorts, unless you are certain that they will be appropriate for your particular hike. Long pants will protect you against bugs, mosquito bites, scrapes against brush and branches, and things like poison ivy. We think that lightweight pants are usually the way to go, and brands we like are Kuhl, Columbia, and Patagonia.

The next thing to consider is the shirt you'll wear. If you are going for an intense hike then you should consider a performance based shirt such as an Under Armour shirt. The goal is to wear something that will keep you comfortable and unsweaty. In mild climates, you want to wear a shirt that is lightweight and will wick away moisture while hiding odors and breathing well. For colder climates you may want to consider wearing long wool shirts. As a beginner you can simply start with your favorite old shirt that you're comfortable in and work on customizing your performance wear later.

Just like with pants, think about the coverage you want on your body, too. Even if the weather is warmer, you may want your shirt to have longer coverage on your arms and more coverage for your neck, to keep bugs and sun off your skin.

Another thing to consider is your jacket. You should pick something that is lightweight so you can pack it on every trip, just in case your need it. The jacket should also be nearly to completely waterproof so you can stay dry during unexpected rain and also heavy enough to block the wind if it gets a little cooler.

Finally, you want to find a good hat. You should choose one with a brim that keeps your ears, neck, and face protected from the sun. The tops of your ears and the back of the neck are the two places most susceptible to getting burned while hiking. Even if you wear a hat that keeps them covered, also make sure to apply sunscreen. When it comes to hats, we like the type that look like an outback hat from Australia with about a 3-4 inch brim all around. It doesn't have to have great shape -- it can be made of anything from hemp to cotton -- it just needs to be durable and help protect you from the sun.

In addition to clothing, your choice of hiking footwear is going to have a major impact on your hiking enjoyment. Finding the right hiking boots might be the single largest investment you make in hiking gear, and it will make a major difference in your ability to cover various types of terrain. Don't skimp on your footwear!

We will spend quite a bit of time next on footwear, because it is so important.

Footwear is both a personal choice as well as a very involved choice to get the best option. For some, the personal preference is over-the-ankle boots while for others it is lightweight trail-running shoes. In addition to personal preference, you will also need to make your decision based on the terrain you're going to be walking on during your hike. If you are hiking well maintained trails then lightweight, low-cut shoes are often fine; but won't do well on a rugged trail with a lot of obstacles such as rocks, roots and streams. No matter what you choose you need to wear footwear that is well broken-in and comfortable when hiking long distances. Plus you need to carefully choose your socks as well. Let's take a look at this important choosing process.

CHOOSING THE BEST SOCKS FOR HIKING *Smart wool*

For the average individual there is 2,000 steps in a mile hike. During each of these steps, the sock you wear play an important part in keeping your feet comfortable and blister free. To choose the right and best socks for your hiking you need to consider four main things:

1. Height: Helps protect your feet against abrasion with your footwear.
2. Cushioning: Determines your comfort and warmth.
3. Fabric: The best hiking socks are made from wool, polyester or nylon.
4. Fit: Appropriate fit helps to prevent blisters.

Let's look at each of these in more detail.

HEIGHT mid calf

Hiking socks come in a range of heights ranging from short that don't even show above the shoes to tall socks that almost go up to your knees. When choosing the right height you need to consider the shoes you plan to wear. The higher the cuffs on your shoes or boots, the taller your socks need to be in order to protect your skin from rubbing against the shoes. There are four specific sock heights you need to consider:

1. No-Show Socks: These socks provide little to no protection against footwear abrasion. They ideally should only be worn with low-cut footwear such as trail running shoes or light hiking shoes.

2. Ankle Socks: These are the next highest socks and often cover the ankle bone for a little more protection. They work best with low to mid-cut shoes or boots.
3. Crew Socks: These are the typical heights for hiking socks. These socks typically land a few inches above the ankle bone and help protect against abrasion with boots that have high cuffs. You can also choose to wear crew socks with low-cut shoes or boots if you want extra coverage, just keep in mind that they can be warm on hot days.
4. Knee High Socks: There are only a few options in this sock category and they are best for mountaineering. Big and/or thick boots can cause abrasions around the calves and shins; but these socks can protect you. The coverage provided by these socks can also keep your lower legs warm if you are climbing in cold weather or hiking at night.

Cushioning and Thickness

The amount of cushioning and thickness in a sock will determine how bulky it is and how warm it will keep your feet. The amount of cushioning you need will depend on the type of hiking you plan to do and the weather you expect to encounter. A small amount of cushion will help protect your feet during high-impact activities such as backpacking and running. However, it is important to remember that thicker socks will cause your feet to sweat and keep them warmer. You are likely going to need to experiment with your socks to find the right balance between cushion and warmth for your needs. It is best to have a variety of socks to choose from to meet each of your hiking needs. There are four levels of cushioning in socks:

1. No Cushioning: These are ultralight socks that are best worn in hot weather since they are very breathable and don't have a lot of padding. These are also sometimes used as liner socks by hikers under lightweight, midweight or heavy weight socks. Liner socks are helpful to wick moisture away from the feet to keep them dry. However, most hiking socks today perform well enough that liner socks aren't necessary anymore.
2. Light Cushioning: These socks are best for warm climates since they focus mostly on moisture wicking and comfort instead of warmth. These socks are pretty thin, but provide cushioning in the right places such as the heel and ball of the foot.
3. Medium Cushioning: These socks provide decent cushioning in the heel and ball of the foot if you are going on extended hikes or backpacking. They also provide enough warmth to wear in cold to moderate climates.

Medium (or more) cushioning can be good for breaking in new hiking boots, because they provide more padding between your skin and the friction points that could cause blisters.
4. Heavy Cushioning: These are the thickest and warmest socks you'll find. They are ideal for long hiking trips in tough terrain and cold climates. They are often too warm and thick for short backpacking trips in hotter climates and are best used when mountaineering or going on cold weather hikes.

FABRIC

Hiking socks are often made from different fabrics rather than a single fabric. It is this blend that creates a good balance of comfort, warmth, durability and drying. There are five common materials in hiking socks:

1. Wool: This is the most popular material for hiking socks and the material that is often recommended over others. Wool is good at regulating temperature so your feet doing get sweaty while also providing adequate cushioning. Wool also has the added benefit of being naturally antimicrobial so it won't hold smells as much as synthetic fabrics. Most hiking socks are made from merino wool, which is nearly itch-free compared to most

types of wool. Also, most hiking socks today have a blend of both wool and synthetic fibers so they dry faster and have better durability.
2. Polyester: This is a synthetic fiber that insulates the feet while wicking away moisture for drying quickly. Polyester is often blended with wool and/or nylon in order to provide the best combination of warmth, comfort, fast drying and durability.
3. Nylon: This is another synthetic fiber that is sometimes used as a primary material. Nylon is durable with a decent drying time.
4. Silk: This material is naturally insulating while being lightweight and comfortable. However, it isn't as durable as other materials. Silk is often used as a material in sock liners because it is a good moisture wicking material.
5. Spandex: Most hiking socks have some percentage of spandex in them. It is this elastic material that helps socks keep their shape and prevent them from bunching and wrinkling.

FIT

Lastly, you want to get socks that fit right in order to keep your feet comfortable while hiking. Socks that are too big will wrinkle, causing rubbing and potentially blisters. Socks that are too small can cause pressure points and slipping.

In order to find the right fit of socks you need to know the size of your actual foot and not your shoe size. People often size-up shoes, which can cause you to buy socks that are too big for your feet. If you don't know your foot size, you can talk to a footwear specialist.

Once you know what your foot size is you can use it on size charts for your socks. If you find yourself between sizes, then it is best to size down in order to avoid excess material that can bunch up and cause your feet to blister.

Lastly, when trying on your socks you want a snug fit that isn't too tight. A proper fitted sock will have a heel cup that lines up with the heel of your foot.

Choosing Hiking Shoes or boots

As with your socks, choosing hiking shoes (or boots, but we will call them shoes for simplicity) is an involved process. The best hiking shoes need to meet with how and where you plan to hike. Before you settle on a shoe, you need to make sure they are the right fit. There are three things to consider:

1. Type: There are a wide range of choices when it comes to hiking shoes; ranging from ultralight trail shoes to mountaineering boots.

2. Components: It is important to know what materials are used in making the uppers, lowers, midsoles, outsoles and other parts of your hiking shoes when making your final selection.
3. Fit: Ill-fitting boots are the difference between getting a blister and enjoying a wonderful time outdoors.

Let's look at each of these three categories to help you choose the right hiking shoe.

TYPES

There are three primary types of hiking shoes to consider:

1. Hiking Shoes: These are low-cut models with a flexible midsole and work best for day hiking. A few experienced ultralight backpackers sometimes even choose to use trail-running shoes for long-distance trips.
2. Day Hiking Boots: These shoes can range from mid- to high-cut styles and are best for day hikes or short backpacking trips that don't require a lot of gear. These shoes often flex easily and don't require a lot of breaking in; but they do lack the support and durability needed for backpacking.
3. Backpacking Boots: These shoes are designed to carry heavy loads or multi-day trips in the

backcountry. Most of these shoes have high cuts that wrap above the ankle to give you the best support. These shocs also have a stiffer midsole than lighter shoes and are suitable for all forms of trail travel.

Components

The material in the upper portion of a hiking boot has an impact on the boot's weight, breathability, durability and water resistance. There are seven materials the upper portion of a hiking boot can be made out of:

1. Full-Grain Leather: This material offers great durability and resistance to abrasions. It also provides good water resistance. You will often find it use in making backpacking boots that are designed for extended trips, heavy gear loads and rugged terrain with many obstacles. However, it isn't as breathable to light as other leather combinations with nylon or split-grain leather. Before wearing these on an extended trip you need to take quite a bit of time to break them in properly.
2. Split-Grain Leather: This material is often paired with nylon or a nylon mesh in order to create a lightweight boot that has good breathability. It is called split-grain leather

because it splits away the rough inner part of the cowhide from the smoother exterior. The benefit to this material is a reduced cost, but it is less durable and water resistant.
3. Nubuck Leather: This is a form of full-grain leather that has been buffed until it looks like suede. It is a durable material that is very resistant to abrasion and water. It is also a flexible material that doesn't require a lot of break in time before you head out on an extended hike.
4. Synthetic Materials: Synthetic materials include polyester, nylon and synthetic leather. Most modern boots use some kind of synthetic material. These boots are often lighter in weight, are easier to break in, dry quicker and are often cheaper. However, they can break down sooner since there is more stitching involved.
5. Waterproof Membranes: Boots and shoes that are labeled as waterproof often have upper portions made from breathable and waterproof membranes to help keep your feet dry in wet conditions. However, these membranes often reduce breathability so your feet are more likely to sweat on hot days.
6. Vegan: This isn't just a category for food. These types of shoes are made without any form of animal by-products or ingredients.

7. Insulation: Some mountaineering boots will have synthetic insulation added to provide warmth to those hiking in cold climates.

Midsoles

The next portion of hiking shoes is the midsoles. This is the area that provides the cushioning for your feet and provides shock absorbing. It is also the area that determines show stiff your shoes are. While stiff shoes may not sound like a comfortable option, they are actually good for those who are going on long hikes over uneven terrain since they provide better stability and comfort. There are two main materials for the midsoles of hiking shoes:

1. EVA or Ethylene Vinyl Acetate: This material provides a little more cushion and is a cheaper material. EVA density can vary to provide you firmer support in certain areas.
2. Polyurethane: This material is often firmer and more durable. It is typically used to make backpacking and mountaineering boots.

Internal Structure

Next you want to consider the material that makes up the internal support of the shoe. There are two things that provide your internal support:

1. Shanks: These are inserts ranging between 3 to 5 mm thick and are placed between the boots' midsoles and outsoles in order to provide the midsole with a load bearing stiffness. Shanks will vary in length with some covering the entire midsole length and others that only cover half.
2. Plates: These inserts are thin and semiflexible. They are placed between the midsoles and outsoles. Sometimes they are included with a shank and placed below them. Plates are helpful for protecting your feet against bruises on uneven surfaces.

Lastly, you want to consider the material of the outsole. All hiking boot outsoles are made from rubber. Although sometimes additives like carbon are used to increase the hardness of mountaineering or backpacking boots. A hard outsole will increase the durability of a shoe, but will also make them more slick if you hike off the trail. There are two specific patterns to a hiking shoe you need to consider:

1. Lug Pattern: These are the traction bumps you see on your boot outsole. The deeper and thicker this pattern is, the better your grip will be. Widely spaced lugs are good for additional traction and make them easier to clean.
2. Heel Brake: This is the heel zone you see clearly defined on hiking shoes. It is distinct

from the arch and forefoot. This feature will help reduce your chance of sliding when having a steep descent.

Fit

The best hiking shoe is one that is snug on your feet everywhere, but also shouldn't be tight and needs to provide room to wiggle your toes. It is best to try them on at the end of the day when your feet have swollen. You also want to try them on wearing the socks you plan to wear while hiking.

For hiking shoes you need to be very specific about your shoe size. You should know your foot's length, width and arch length. Ideally these three need to be measured with a specially calibrated fit device. Stand on the insoles of your boots and you should find that you have a thumb's width of space between the longest toe and the end of your insole.

In is best to try on your hiking shoes at the end of the day. Feet typically swell after a day of activity and are their largest at night. Trying shoes on late in the day will prevent you from buying hiking boots that are too small for your feet.

If you wear any sort of orthotics you should bring them when trying on hiking boots as they will impact the overall fit of the boot.

You should also wear the right socks when trying on your hiking boots. Socks you are familiar with will make it easier to assess the fit and feel of your new hiking boots. The thickness of the socks should match that of the ones you intend to wear on the trail.

Take some time to walk around the store in the boots. If available be sure to go up and down stairs or find an inclined surface to walk on and see how the boots feel.

With the best fitting hiking boot you should feel no odd bumps or seams, no pinching in the forefoot, no toes hitting the end of the boot when you're on an incline and no space at the top of your foot.

Once you find a good pair of hiking boots or shoes that fit you well and feel good on the trail, we suggest sticking with that brand for future purposes. Each manufactuer has a different way of designing and assembling boots and shoes, and your foot will naturally fit best with one of them. You can also choose to purchase aftermarket insoles to help with the comfort, support and fit of your hiking boot. Lastly, make sure you break in your shoes before heading out on your first hike.

Step 4

Choosing the Right Hiking Gear

One of the best things about hiking as a form of exercise is that it doesn't require you to purchase a lot of equipment or high-tech gear. Often for a short trip you don't need to pack anything, but for safety and preparedness you should at least pack the eleven essentials when heading out for a hike.

The Eleven Essentials

The eleven essentials is a collection of gear that everyone should carry before heading out on the hiking trail. Even if you are only going on a short day hike, carrying these eleven essentials is important since they will help you be prepared for nearly any situation you face on the trail. Consider the following table to see how the eleven essentials vary for short to long hikes.

Essential	Up to 4 Hour Hike	Over 4 Hour Hike
Navigation	Local Map	Local Map Compass
Sun Protection	Sunscreen Hat Sunglasses	Sunscreen Hat Sunglasses Long Sleeved Shirt
Insulation	Sweater/Jacket	Sweater/Jacket

	Rain Jacket and Pants	Rain Jacket and Pants
		Beanie Hat
		Insulated Jacket
Illumination	Headlamp	Headlamp
	Extra Batteries	Extra Batteries
First Aid Kit	Medical Kit	Medical Kit
Fire	Matches	Matches
	Fire Steel	Fire Steel
	Vaseline Coated Cotton Balls	Vaseline Coated Cotton Balls
Repair Kit and Tools	Swiss Army Knife	Swiss Army Knife
	Duct Tape	Duct Tape
	Safety Pins	Safety Pins
Nutrition	Nuts, Dried Fruit, Bars	Nuts, Dried Fruit, Bars
		Sandwiches
Bug Protection	DEET-based bug spray or lotion	Ability to re-apply every 4-6 hours
Hydration	2 Water Bottles	2 Water Bottles
		Water purification tablets or Water filter
Emergency Shelter	Emergency Bivy	Emergency Bivy
		Foam Sit Pad
		Tarp and Paracord

Let's consider these in a little more detail, to see why you really need to carry this much gear when you are simply heading out for a hike.

NAVIGATION

Two of the main components of navigation are the map and compass. However, you can go a step further and carry an altimeter, a GPS and other items.

Any trip that is more than a short, well-marked footpath or a well traveled nature path needs to have a topographic map. In addition, to map-reading knowledge; a vital tool is to have a compass. These can help if you get disoriented in the backcountry.

Other options include carrying a high-tech GPS receiver. However, this doesn't mean you shouldn't skip carrying and learning to use a compass. A compass is lightweight and doesn't require you to carry batteries. You can also use a compass as a sighting mirror in case you need to signal during an emergency.

Lastly, you can consider bringing an altimeter as a navigational extra. These use a barometric sensor to measure air pressure and provide you with an estimate of your elevation. This can help you track your progress while also help determine your location on a map.

Many people ask: Can't I just use my phone for navigation? The answer is that you should not rely primarily on a phone for two reasons. First, reception is often limited or non-existent in hiking areas. Second, factors such as cold, rain, and roaming mode may drain your battery abnormally fast, leaving you without anything to navigate with.

Sun Protection

Sun protection is very important if you are going to be outdoors for any period of time. Sunglasses that block 100% ultraviolet light both UVA and UVB are important and if you are going to be hiking in snow or ice then you should get extra-dark glacier sunglasses.

It is also important to have appropriate sunscreen. According to health experts you should choose a sunscreen that offers an SPF factor of at least 15, but 30 is recommended for extended outdoor activity. You also want to get a sunscreen that blocks both UVA and UVB rays. Depending on a range of factors including the time of day and how much you sweat, you should ideally reapply your sunscreen every 2 hours. It is also a good idea to wear some SPF-rated lip balm as well.

For a longer hike you may also want to consider some sun-protection clothing that provide ultraviolet protection factor. Whether you choose to wear pants or shorts will depend on your activity level and how much you perspire. If you plan to wear shorts or short-sleeved shirts then you should remember to apply sunscreen to all exposed skin areas.

INSULATION

When you are in the wilderness the weather conditions can change abruptly. You can suddenly find yourself in a downpour or under windy, cold conditions. This is why it is best to carry an extra layer of clothing in case you are exposed to the elements for longer than expected. Expert hikers recommend asking yourself what you need to survive the worst conditions you may experience on the trip and then pack accordingly. Some typical options include an extra layer of underwear, an insulating hat, extra socks and a synthetic jacket.

ILLUMINATION

When hiking the preferred choice for illumination is headlamps since they allow hands-free operation while being lightweight and have a long battery life. Most headlamps come with a strobe mode so you can also use them in an emergency. You can also choose to carry flashlights and packable lanterns. No matter what you choose it is also a good idea to carry spare batteries as well.

FIRST-AID SUPPLIES

You can choose to get a pre-assembled first-aid kit so you don't have to struggle with building your own, but sometimes it is best to personalize your first-aid kit for your own needs. The basics that you should include in a first-aid kit include the following:

- Blister treatments
- Adhesive bandages in varying sizes
- Gauze pads
- Adhesive tape
- Disinfecting ointment
- Over-the-counter pain medication
- Pen and paper
- Nitrile gloves

The length of your hiking trip and the number of people involved will have the greatest impact on any additional contents of your first-aid kit. You may also want to consider carrying a compact guide for medical emergencies.

Fire

Before heading out on a hike you at least want to carry some waterproof matches or regular matches stored in a waterproof container. You can carry a mechanical lighter, but it is always best to carry matches as a backup. You may also want to consider carrying a fire starter. It is best to choose one that ignites quickly and sustains heat for a few seconds or more.

Tools and Repair Kit

Carrying a knife or multi-tool can be very helpful when hiking. They work for repair, food preparation, first aid and other emergency needs. The basic multi-tool should at least have 1 fold out knife blade, 1 to 2 flathead screwdrivers, a can opener and a pair of fold out scissors. The more complex your needs, the more tools you may want to carry.

For example, if you are going on a backpacking trip with a self-inflating mattress then you should consider packing a repair kit for it.

Nutrition

We'll discuss more about food for hiking in the next chapter. However, it is best to always pack an extra day worth of food. This can be a freeze-dried meal or any no cook items that have a long storage time such as energy bars, nuts, dried fruits or jerky. The process of digesting will help keep your body warm so it is important to have this extra source of fuel on hand if you end up outside longer than expected.

Bug Protection

Bug protection is needed in many parts of the country. The assumption is that you want to protect from bugs in order to be comfortable outside. While that is correct, the more important reason for protecting yourself from bugs is that many mosquitoes and ticks can transmit diseases to humans. If you are in an area with mosquitoes, be sure to use DEET-based products to keep them away. If you are in an area known to have ticks, such as the blacklegged tick which carries Lyme disease, consider also using permethrin on your shoes, socks, and clothing to discouring them from hitching a ride on you.

Hydration

Again, we will discuss this more in the next chapter. However, it can't be stated enough how important proper hydration is when outdoors hiking. You should always carry at least one water bottle and a collapsible water reservoir. For a longer hike you should also carry some form of water treatment whether it be a filter/purifier or chemical treatment. You can also consult your map and identify any sources of possible water.

EMERGENCY SHELTER

Shelter is something relatively new to the essential item list for hikers. If you are going on a backpacking trip you will likely already be carrying a tent or tarp. However, this isn't something more day hikers bring with them. Although if you get lost or injured then it is best to have something to protect your from the rain or wind. Consider carrying an ultralight tarp, a bivy sack or an emergency space blanket. The thing is to pack something small and lightweight that can help protect you from the elements.

In addition to these eleven essentials, there may be some additional items that you'll want to carry based on your individual needs and hiking location. For example, you may want to carry some insect repellent in the form of a lotion or spray.
A whistle is a good item to carry for potential emergencies if you need to signal for help. The ultimate in signalling would be to carry a personal locator beacon, especially if you are hiking in the

far wilderness. Another added safety feature is a two-way radio, a cell phone or satellite phone; make sure they are fully charged before you head out and carry a spare battery or other solar charging option.

Finally, you need to carry your ten essential items and any other gear you need. For short hikes close to home you will likely only need a daypack that has the ability to carry about 15 to 20 liters and give you enough space for water, some snacks and a lightweight layer of clothing. If you need to carry more gear or are planning a longer hiking trip you'll need a pack that has a 30 liter capacity.

Test out the packs, and make sure they fit comfortably on your body. Some packs focus the weight on the shoulders, others on the waist. Some packs spread the weight out on the back, while others are more concentrated on one spot. Some hikers like a pack with an easy-access spot for a water bottle, while others really prefer that everything is contained inside the compartments. It is really personal preference based on how you feel most comfortable.

Do you like what you are reading so far? Do you find this information useful? Consider leaving a review at

https://www.amazon.com/dp/B07D94B4S9

It would mean a lot to me!

Now, back to the 7 Steps.....

STEP

5

Choosing and Preparing Food and Water

When you first start out hiking it can be very difficult to know how much food and water to bring. The amount of calories you will expend on a hike various based on your conditioning, normal eating habits, and the terrain of the hike.

The general rule of thumb is to eat 200-300 calories per hour for food and about a half liter per hour of moderate activity in moderate temperature for water. The amount of food and water will depend on several factors such as the hike intensity, the weather, your age, your sweat rate and your body type. Once you get more experience you will gain a better sense of how much food and water you need. No matter what you need, it is important that you carry a little extra food and water in case something comes up and your hike takes longer.

No matter what shape you are in or what type of hike you are doing, food and water is needed in order to fuel your body and keep it working at peak performance. While you can choose to eat traditional food and simply drink water; energy foods and drinks provide you with a few extra advantages including the following:

- Portability
- Digestibility
- Convenience
- Long shelf life

This presents the new hiker with a greater problem. There is no shortage of energy foods and drinks to choose from, so how can you know you are making the right choice. There are four things you need to take into consideration when choosing what energy foods and drinks to take with you on a hike.

1. Nutritional Information: Including calories, fat, carbs and protein.
2. When to Eat: Some food and drink is designed for consumption before, during and/or after a hike.
3. Types: Including bars, gels, bites and chews for food and sport or recovery drinks.
4. Features: Such as organic, vegan, vegetarian, gluten-free and non-GMO.

Nutritional Information

Before choosing energy foods and drinks, it is best to have some basic nutritional information. You should consider the following.

The number of calories you need to consume per hour depends on several factors, including the length and intensity of your hike as well as your body type. A general number is 200 to 300 calories per hour. Most energy bars, gels, bites and drinks are made to fall within this range and you can eat them as directed on the package.

Your main energy source is carbohydrates. The higher your activity level and duration, the more carbohydrates you are typically going to need to consume. Most people have a limit of processing 60 grams of carbohydrates per hour and eating or drinking more than this can lead to an upset stomach.

Protein is an important nutritional ingredient since it helps rebuild tissues and allows your body to recover after any activity and/or exercise. Protein can also help to sustain energy if you have a long hike that requires endurance.

Most energy foods are low in fats. Only energy foods designed as meal replacements or those specifically designed for endurance will have more fat in them.

Sodium is an important electrolyte. It helps to metabolize your carbohydrates to help keep your muscles functioning properly and also works to help keep you hydrated.

Potassium is another electrolyte that is just as important as sodium in metabolizing carbohydrates.

Vitamins and minerals are naturally burned by your body during activity and/or exercise, so a lot of energy products include them. Energy bars typically have a high number of vitamins and minerals.

Energy gels often have the addition of amino acid blends such as leucine, valine and isoleucine. These are basically a form of protein that is broken down by the body and used to help build muscles and keep them in shape.

Some bars, gels and drinks contain caffeine to help give you extra energy. Products enhanced with caffeine are often clearly marked so you can avoid products with this if you don't want to have added caffeine.

WHEN TO EAT

Energy foods and drinks are designed to enhance specific stages of an outdoor hike: before, during and after. This allows you to fine tune your nutritional intake.

Foods or drinks formulated to be consumed before activity help by providing an elevated, consistent energy level over an extended period of time. Often they have a balanced mix of carbohydrates, proteins and fiber. It is often recommended to consume them with a lead time of about one to two hours before activity begins; particularly if there is fat and protein in it. Most energy bars fit into this category.

Foods or drinks formulated to be consumed during activity are designed for easy digestion and absorption. The goal of these foods and drinks is to provide you with sustained energy through a gradual increase in energy rather than a spike and a subsequent gradual decline. Chews, gels and beverages are preferred because they are simple.

Foods or drinks formulated to be consumed after activity are designed mostly for recovery. They often have a number of proteins, amino acids and other elements to help restore muscles and increase cell repair within your body. Bars, drinks and supplements are popular forms of post activity energy foods and drinks.

As a general rule, always try to eat a little prior to actually feeling hungry or thirsty. By the time you actual feel hunger or thirst, your body is probably going in to efficiency mode, and your performance is likely declining.

TYPES

The biggest category is energy bars. With so many options to choose from you are sure to find a bar that you not only enjoy the taste of, but also something that meets your nutritional needs. Most bars are high in carbohydrates, low in protein and fat; a good combination for before activity consumption. The high grade carbohydrates in these bars give you a good endurance boost during a hike and then help replenish muscle reserves after the hike. If your stomach can tolerate solid food during activity and you're going to be hiking more than a few hours, energy bars are a great way to introduce protein and fat into your diet to give you sustained energy. A few types of energy bars provide large amounts of protein to help your body rebuild tissue and recover after a hike. When eating an energy bar it is a good idea to drink water. Most energy bars are typically dense and chewy so they become easier to digest with a lot of water. Avoid drinking a performance beverage with energy bars since consuming too much carbohydrates will slow your body's ability to absorb them properly.

Energy gels are popular among hikers as an on-the-go snack. They are semi-liquid products that are often high in carbohydrates to provide easy to digest energy and electrolytes to replace what is lost during a hike. Gel packets are small and light so they are easy to carry while hiking. Any activity that lasts over three hours can use energy gels to keep going. For longer hikes you may need to combine the gel with an energy bar and/or drink to add some fat and protein to the mix. As with energy bars, you want to drink plenty of water with energy gels.

If you don't like the texture of energy gels then you can consider trying bites or chews. You can find these in a range of consistencies ranging from gummy bears to jelly beans. Bites and chews have the same functional purpose as gels by giving you the needed carbohydrates and electrolytes. These are typically designed to be consumed while hiking, but on longer hikes they will need to be combined with energy bars and/or drinks. As with everything else, drinking water will help with digestion.

When it comes to drink mixes you have two options. The first is sport drinks. These drinks are designed to replace lost electrolytes while sweating on a hike. The major electrolytes sodium, potassium, calcium and magnesium play a major role in the bodies healthy functioning heart, nerves and muscles. If your electrolytes run low you will feel tired and your performance may drop. A few sports drinks will also have caffeine, carbohydrates and/or protein to provide extra energy. Other drinks have a high amount of calories. These drinks are a good option for those who have trouble eating solid food while on a hike. You may have to experiment with drinks first to find one that works well for you and has a taste you prefer.

A second option is recovery drinks. These are drinks high in protein to help with recovery and are designed to be drank after a hike. Providing your muscles with protein after a high can help them to recovery quicker.

Lastly, you have the option of taking supplements. This can be an easy way to add vitamins, nutrients and electrolytes without added calories. You can find a variety of benefits with supplements depending on your nutritional needs. Just make sure you follow directions on the packaging for proper use.

WATER

The average human body is made up of 60 percent water and even light exercise can deplete this; leading to a down feeling and a decrease in your performance. No matter how long or strenuous your hike you need to make sure your properly hydrate.

First, you want to consider how much to drink. The amount you need to drink depends on several factors including the following:

- Activity
- Intensity
- Duration
- Weather
- Age
- Sweat rate
- Body type

A general recommendation is about a half liter of water per hour of moderate activity in a moderate temperature climate. You will need to increase the amount you drink if the temperature or intensity increases. As you get out and hike more you'll be able to fine tune the amount you need to drink.

The hiking you are doing will likely determine where you keep your water, but it is important to keep it close at hand. A great option for hiking is to have a hydration reservoir. If you prefer using a water bottle you want to keep it someplace accessible such as a side pocket on your backpack.

Rather than chugging water, it is better to take small sips of water to stay continually hydrated.

Keep in mind that when you sweat you lose electrolytes and when you lose too much your performance starts to suffer. If your hike is going to last an hour or less then you probably aren't going to have to worry about losing electrolytes, but if you are going to be hiking any longer then you need to make sure you compensate for electrolyte loss. The two most important electrolytes to replace is sodium and potassium, but you also want to consider calcium and magnesium. The easiest solution is through a sport drink. You can also choose to purchase powders and tablets that you can mix with your water.

When hiking at higher altitude you are also at greater risk of dehydration. You are also less likely to crave water and feel thirsty when at higher altitudes. This means it is even more important to drink frequently.

If you're hiking on a colder day, you may not feel like drinking cold water; but it is still important to stay hydrated. If you need, pack a hot drink to help you stay hydrated when hiking in the cold.

It can be a good idea to pre-hydrate before heading out on your hike. It is a good idea to drink about 17 to 20 fluid ounces about two hours before starting your hike.

After hiking (or any physical activity) it is important to rehydrate. Even when you have not been sweating, you have likely been processing fluids and hydration is important. When you get your fluid levels back to normal your body will be able to recover easier. This is sometimes as simple as drinking a glass of water when you get home. However, if you want to be specific then you can drink 16 to 24 fluid ounces of water per pound you lose during hiking.

It is also important that you plan your hiking route if you are going on an extended hike. Water can weigh a lot and if you don't want to carry the extra weight then you can plan a route that will take your to places where you can refill your water bottle. Another option is to bring a water filter and refill from a lake or stream.

Lastly, remember to protect yourself from sunburn. Getting sunburned can speed up dehydration. So make sure you take all precautions against the sun.

Since hydration is such an important issue it is important to recognize the risks and signs of dehydration as well as over hydration.

Dehydration is what happens when the body loses fluids through sweating and fluids aren't consumed in appropriate amounts. Once you feel thirsty, dehydration has already started. If you don't drink water to counteract this then the body will continue to provide signs of dehydration.

Early signs include:

- Thirst
- Dry mouth
- Energy decrease

Later symptoms of dehydration include:

- Cramps
- Headaches
- Nausea
- Stumbling
- Mumbling
- Grumbling
- Fumbling
- Dark urine with less volume
- Decline in performance

The solution to dehydration is as simple as drinking water. It is better to take small sips frequently rather than chugging large amounts infrequently. You can also drink sports/energy drinks to help replenish electrolytes and carbohydrates.

By the time you begin to displays signs of dehydration, you have already lost a step. The best cure is prevention -- drink regularly, and sip water along the way, even before you feel thristy. Just make it part of every break you take.

You can monitor your water intake by weighing before and after hiking. Ideally you should weight the same. If you find you've lost several pounds then you're likely not drinking enough water while hiking. For each pound you lose you should drink 16 to 24 fluid ounces and plan to drink more water on your next hike.

Dehydration isn't the only concern, you also have to be concerned with overhydration or hyponatremia. This is a rare condition and typically only affects endurance athletes. In the case of over hydration, sodium levels become so diluted that the function of cells are impaired. In extreme cases, it can lead to coma and death. The symptoms are similar to dehydration including:

- Fatigue
- Headache
- Nausea

This is why some people falsely think they are dehydrated and drink more, making the issue worse. The key to preventing over hydration is to monitor your fluid intake.

The first thing to do is to not overdrink. Stick to drinking about 10 fluid ounces every 20 minutes and try to avoid drinking more than you're sweating. Gaining weight after hiking is a sign that you are drinking too much.

Second, you need to keep your salt levels balanced, especially on hot, sunny days. Do this by occasionally drinking a sports drink that contains electrolytes rather than plain water. You can also help by eating a salty snack or taking salt tablets.

STEP 6

Preparing for Hiking Safety and Emergencies

It is important that you learn outdoor skills and know how to stay safe while hiking. You can do this through research by reading a guide like this or others, taking an online or in person wilderness class or by hiking with an experienced person. No matter how experienced you become, the most important safety step you can take is to tell family or friends about your plans and what to do if they don't hear from you at a designated time.

Let's look at a few other safety tips to help you stay safe out on the trail.

Hiking in the Winter

Just because it is winter doesn't mean you can't go hiking. Hiking in the winter and snow can be both a beautiful and refreshing experience, with fewer people on the trail which gives you more solitude. However, there are additional safety challenges to take into consideration. If you plan to hike in the winter or snow then you should consider the following tips:

- Dress in layers and be sure to pack extra layers.

- Avoid wearing anything made from cotton since this can hasten the onset of hypothermia if you get wet.
- Learn to recognize signs and symptoms of hypothermia, frostbite and trench foot.
- Never hike alone in the winter and ideally hike with someone more experienced than you.
- Before heading out, make sure you research the trail and presents no avalanche danger. If there is a risk of avalanche then research how to travel in avalanche territory.
- Since snow can easily obscure the trail, it is important that you know how to read a topographic map and compass.
- Winter has fewer daylight hours, so you should make sure your hike is finished before nightfall. Just in case you find yourself out after dark, make sure you pack a headlamp and/or flashlight.

Additionally, do not rely on your mobile phone for safety in winter. Because of the cold, the battery life will be much shorter than it would in summer temps.

With the above tips and the right preparation, winter hiking can be a wonderful experience. The same can be said for hiking in the summer months.

Hiking in the Summer

In many places, summer is the best time to hike. The days are longest, the temps are often comfortable, and the vegetation is in prime growing season. However, in other parts of the country; hiking outdoors in the summer is like hiking in an oven. Summers can be deadly, especially when you combine physical activity with high temperatures. Hiking in the summer can lead to complications such as dehydration, heat exhaustion, heat stroke and even death -- if you choose the wrong trail and are ill-prepared for it. If you are going to hike on a hot day make sure you are prepared to protect yourself from the high temperature and be aware of danger signs. This means you need to take it a step further than drinking water and applying sunscreen.

Read a Map and Use a Compass

Getting lost or disoriented on hikes can happen, even one well marked and popular trails. It is important that you know how to read a map and use a compass before you head out on your first hike.

When it comes to map reading, it is important that you learn to use topographic maps. These maps show geographic features and use contour lines to show you changes in the earth's surface like valleys and mountains. Contour lines show you how steep a mountain is or how sharp of a drop the trail takes. Topographic maps are different from road maps or a simple trail map and it is important that you learn how to read one before hiking.

Some hikers choose to purchase a hiking GPS when heading out on a complex hike or a backcountry travel. A GPS is a great navigational tool to have and they can provide a lot of information; but you shouldn't rely simply on your GPS. Technology can fail and a map never will.

WATER PURIFICATION

It is important that you always bring more water on a hike than you think you'll actually need. For a short hike, this is an easy rule to follow. However, as your hike increase in length and difficulty you'll want to start considering how you can purify water from lakes and streams to increase your safe drinking water sources.

Water is a heavy item. When you use a known water source along the trail then you are able to lighten your pack significantly. It is also a good survival skill to know how to purify water while on the trail.

What to Do If You Get Lost

There are a few things you can do while hiking that will make it easier to find your way back to the start later:

- Always look out for easily identifiable landmarks.
- Take photos while you hike, not only will you get good memories but you'll also have a way to remember the trail and find your way back to where you started.
- If you really want to be prepared against getting lost then you can build small arrows or cairns with rocks or sticks. These identifiers can be left and help you to find your way back to your starting point. Just make sure you destroy them on your way back.

If you do find yourself lost while hiking then follow the US Forest Service recommendation called STOP: Stop, Think, Observe and Plan.

Stop as soon as you know you're lost, don't try to keep moving around the area. Rather stay calm and avoid panicking. The reason you stop is because you are already disoriented, and continuing to walk in a semi-panicked state could just get you more lost. The fewer steps you take, the closer you are to the original trail that you intended to be on.

Think before you move. Retrace the route you took in your mind. Think about any landmarks you passed. Look through any photos you've taken. Lastly, don't make any move until you've relaxed and had time to think through your situation with a clear head.

Observe your surroundings. If you are on a trail, stay on the trail since you are clearly on a path that will take you somewhere. If you have a compass, use it to get a better understanding of where you are. If you must, follow a stream or drainage that goes downhill. This can be a dangerous and wrong decision, but in a pinch can often lead you to a road or trail.

Plan your next course of action based on the steps above; if you aren't confident in your plan then stay put until you can have a solid route planned. If it is after dark or you are extra tired then it can be a good idea to just stay put until morning. Sunrise always makes it easier to make rational decisions and think clearer. However, this then brings up the idea of what you need to do if you find you have to stay outdoors overnight.

If you find yourself in need of staying overnight outdoors then there are four things you need to do.

1. Find a shelter as soon as possible. You can either find a natural area to stay or you can

use a shelter you pack with you. The goal is to protect yourself from wind and rain. It is best to do this before the sun sets.
2. If you have packed extra layers, put them on in order to prevent hypothermia.
3. If needed, start a small fire to keep warm. The smoke signals will help as well. However, make sure you control the fire since you don't want to cause a forest fire.
4. Hang colorful items from the nearby tree branches so you will be easily seen from above by search and rescue crews.

If morning comes and you find you're still lost and no one has found you yet, then you need to be prepared to survive for a few days until search and rescue crews can find you. This isn't easy, but there are a few simple things to do to increase your chances of surviving.

The most important thing to do is prevent thirst. The average human can survive up to three weeks without food, but only three days without water. Therefore, it is important that the first thing you do in order to survive is find a hydration source.

The second thing you need to do is prevent exhaustion. If you become tired it will lead to you making poor decisions. Therefore, any time you feel fatigued it is important that you take a nap.

It is also important that you stay warm and dry. Unless you are looking at the ideal warm spring day with a comfortable 24-hour period, there is a chance you'll become cold or hot. Neither of these temperatures is good since it can lead to hypothermia or dehydration and heat sickness. In hot weather, prevent yourself from sweating too much by keeping your clothes from soaking in your sweat.

It is important to avoid infection as much as possible. While a broken limb is bad, a small cut can be worse if it leads to a major infection. Make sure you clean and wash any wounds in order to prevent an infection from worsening.

As we mentioned earlier, you also want to prevent hunger. While you can go a while without food; your body will become weak. You need to find a food source in order to keep your strength up. So make sure you keep up your intake of calories.

Lastly, make sure you do what you can to prevent fear and loneliness from overwhelming you. More than anything, when lost your human emotions will get the best of you. It can be hard to not get scared, but do your best to remain calm. Fear and loneliness will only compound the situation. If needed, keep yourself busy with daily tasks to keep you focused.

No one ever dreams of getting lost and when you are a beginner hiker on a well-marked path; it definitely shouldn't happen. However, if you are going to spend any time outdoors then you want to be prepared for worst case scenarios. Using the above tips will help you if the worst case does happen. Just do your research on the area in advance and you can reduce your risk of getting lost.

FIRST AID WHILE HIKING

When you go hiking, it is always important to carry a first aid kit with you. You should make sure it is well stocked and specialized to meet your specific needs. Most of all you need to make sure you know how to use all your first aid supplies. Be prepared to handle a range of medical situations. Some common issues you may experience while hiking that you should research treatments for include the following:

- Blisters
- Allergic reactions
- Poisonous plants
- Insect bites or stings
- Cuts
- Sprained ankle

I'll leave you to research most of these on your own since the list of specific concerns is going to vary based on your health, body type and location of hiking. However, I want to talk to you about the most common injury that all hikers will face at some point: blisters.

BLISTERS

A simple foot blister is one of the most common injuries a hiker suffers. Thankfully there is a lot of information on preventing and treating blisters. There are three main ways that you can deal with blisters:

1. Know the cause of blisters such as pressure, heat and moisture.
2. Prevent blisters from forming in the first place. Make sure you have proper fitting hiking boots, wear proper socks and take care of any potential blister spots right away by covering them with a padded blister bandage, moleskin or tape.
3. Care for blisters right away before they have a chance to worsen. Avoid draining your blister is possible and protect it by cutting a blister sized hole in a piece of mole foam.

The most common culprit of blisters is friction; but they can also be caused by burns, allergies, skin conditions and even spider bites. Enough friction on a specific focused spot will cause cell damage. A blister fills with serum or fluid in order to healt the damaged tissue. A blood blister fills with red fluid because the capillaries in the area are also damaged. There are a few factors that make blisters more likely:

Pressure. Any tight spot in your hiking boots or a wrinkle in your sock can cause a friction pressure point.

Direct Friction. Any time a shearing force grabs the skin and slides it can develop a blister. This will often happen in the heel of a hiking boot or in a glove when you grip the shaft of a tool or walking stick. Eventually the upper layer of your skin called the epidermis separates and allows fluid to enter the space, developing into a blister.

Moisture. Skin that is moist will be softer, such as when you sweat. This softer skin is more susceptible to damage once there is friction.

The key to preventing blisters is vigilance and awareness. Once you know the factors that increase your chance of getting blisters then you can watch for them and reduce their chances. There are a few guidelines you need to follow in order to prevent blisters from forming while out hiking.

The first thing you must do is make sure your hiking boots fit properly and are appropriately broken in before wearing them on the trail. This will ensure you don't have pressure points, slipping or both.

Along these lines you also want to make sure you wear proper socks. The number one rule when hiking is to avoid wearing cotton socks. Cotton will retain moisture. Rather wear synthetic or wool socks and make sure they fit properly. Socks that are too big will have wrinkles and socks that are too small will have pressure points and slipping. In addition there are a few things you want to do to improve your socks.

Consider wearing liner socks as these will provide an extra protective layer between your skin and your main hiking socks. In addition, a liner sock will help wick away moisture.

You also want to change to dry socks frequently. Fresh socks can reduce the moisture level of your feet and should definitely be changed whenever your feet get wet.

If your feet have an area that is prone to blisters or is at risk of blisters then make sure you treat the area quickly. Monitor how your feet feel while you hike. The moment you feel an uncomfortable spot, you should stop and take your hiking boots and sock off to treat the area. There are plenty of blister kits on the market that can help with the prevention and treatment of blisters. Some of the types of kits you may find are the following:

Tape. This is an inexpensive way to prevent and treat blisters. Paper surgeon's tape is effective since you can tear to the needed size and it has a gentle adhesive. You can also use kinetic tapes, cloth and synthetic medical tapes as well as duct tape in a pinch.

Blister Bandages with Pads and Gels. These products can be used on hot spots to help prevent blisters as well as for treatment of blisters once they've formed.

Moleskin. These are the classed blister coverage products that can be cut to size. They have the advantage of being durable and stick will to the blister. There are plenty of similar products on the market with a range of different names.

If a blister does develop then you have several treatment options to consider.

The best option is mole foam with a donut hole. Simply cut a hole large enough for the blister and the surrounding foam will then prevent your sock from rubbing and irritating the area further. If you want an extra layer of protection you can add a layer of moleskin or tape over the area.

Another option is to use the blister bandages with pads and gels. These give you a protective layer that prevents the blister from getting worse. The pads have a built in cushion and the gel will soothe the area by cooling it.

If necessary you can drain the blister. If possible you want to avoid opening the blister and releasing the fluid. When you open a blister you are increasing the chance of an infection and you would be removing the protection and healing properties of the serum. However, if you have a large blister that is too painful to leave undrained then you need to do a few steps to properly pop the blister. If it pops on its own you can skip to step four.

1. Use an antibiotic soap to wash the blister and the area around it.
2. Sterilize a needle with heat or alcohol.
3. Poke the base of the blister with the needle.
4. Dress the blister similar to a wound with antibiotic ointment and gauze or a Band-Aid.
5. Cut and place molefoam with a donut hole around the area to avoid additional irritation. Fill the hole with antibiotic ointment or a blister pad for added protection and place a layer of tape over the top.

While blisters rarely get infected, you should always keep a close eye on blisters. If the area develops redness, pain, pus or red streaks traveling towards your lymph nodes then you should leave the trail immediately and head for the nearest medical care.

STEP 7

The Hike - Proper Etiquette

Whether you're heading out for your first hike or you've been hiking or years; it is important that you know and follow proper etiquette. 95% of hikers abide by an unwritten (and in some cases written) code that allows everyone to enjoy the trails, with minimal impact to the environment or each other. Unfortunately, 5% of hikers ignore this code, and they can affect the experience for everyone.

Strive to be a good citizen in the hiking community. Let's look at some of the common trail etiquette you should follow.

Right of Way

Everyone can get a long a lot easier by observing right of way rules:

Hikers versus Hikers. Those going uphill have the right of way. It is the uphill hikers decision to let others come downhill while they take a break, but right of way is always given to uphill hikers.

Hikers versus Bikers. Mountain bikers should always yield to hikers. However, since bikers are often traveling faster than hikers it is often easier for the hiker to step out of the way and yield right of way.

Hikers versus Horses. Horses always get the right of way. If you're sharing the trail with a horse you want to give them a wide berth and avoid making any abrupt movements. It is often recommended that you step off the trail on the downhill side while yielding to horses.

LEAVE NO TRACE

While most people who go hiking don't intend to harm nature and often hike because they want to become one with their natural surroundings; you also need to make sure you know how to preserve our beautiful outdoor area. You may be surprised that you've overlooked a few important behaviors that help to preserve the great outdoors. The seven basic principles to follow while hiking are the following:

1. Prepare and plan ahead for your hike
2. Hike and camp only on durable surfaces
3. Properly dispose of all waste, which often means packing it back out with you
4. Leave everything you find and only take pictures
5. Minimize the impacts of any campfires
6. Respect all wildlife; do not feed or approach it
7. Be considerate of other hikers around you, minimizing noise and impact

Give Back

If you find that you enjoy hiking as much as we think you will, consider giving back to the hiking community and the nature that you enjoy so much. There are a few ways to do that, including:

- Trail clean-up days. A trail cleanup day is often done with volunteer labor. The goal is to get out on a favorite trail and pick up any litter, cut vegetation back, and repair the trail surface, if needed. It is a great way to get to know fellow hikers in addition to taking care of a favorite trail. Look for local groups, often named "friends of the ABC trial' for times on clean-up events.
- Support foundations. Many of those same "trail friends" groups are nonprofits who accept donations in order to maintain trails. Consider supporting them, they are often the critical link to trail upkeep as well as blazing new trails.
- Bring a kid hiking. The future of hiking, and proper trail appreciation, depends on every generation creating new experiences and appreciation for the outdoors. If you have children in your life, introduce them to hiking. Do it gradually at first, and keep it fun.
- Leave reviews. Leaving reviews on popular trail websites will help other hikers learn about the trails in a particular area.

Now you are prepared and ready to hit the trail. Enjoy your time and soon you'll be looking at longer and more advanced backpacking trips.

A Note From the Author

If you enjoyed this guide and found it useful, please consider leaving a review on Amazon. Your review would mean a lot to me, thank you! You can leave your review here: https://www.amazon.com/Hiking-Beginners-Steps-Becoming-Capable-ebook/dp/B07QF2YRDT

Resources

Below are some of our favorite resources for hikers.

All Trails: https://www.alltrails.com/ A resource for researching and reviewing trails, with more than 60,000 trails in the database

Tick and Mosquito Project: https://control-mosquitoes.com A group devoted to providing useful information on preventing tick and mosquito bites, which can sometimes be quite dangerous

Recreation.gov: https://www.recreation.gov/ The federal government's resource for reserving campsites and permits, and other outdoors information. Over 3,500 federally-owned sites are included at the website.

National Weather Service: https://www.weather.gov/ Our go-to resource for finding information on weather, fires, floods, and everything in-between, helping to ensure you are hiking in safe conditions

Made in the USA
Monee, IL
26 August 2022